HISTORIC HOMES
of
NEW ENGLAND

Author
Bill Harris

Editors
Gill Waugh
Pauline Graham

Commissioning Editor
Trevor Hall

Designer
Teddy Hartshorn

Photography
Ric Pattison
Chris Swan

Production Director
Gerald Hughes

Publishing Director
David Gibbon

Acknowledgments

The publisher wishes to thank all the many individuals and
organizations who so readily gave their assistance during the
preparation of this book. Special thanks are due to the
owners and keepers of the featured homes, and in particular
the following:

Margherita M. Desy, Curator, Harriet Beecher Stowe House, Hartford, CN..
The Webb-Deane-Stevens Museum, Wethersfield, CN.
William Lyman, Acting Chairman of the Warner House Association, Portsmouth, N.H.
The Society for the Preservation of New England Antiquities, Boston, MA..
The Mark Twain Memorial, Hartford, CN.
The Friends of Hildene, Inc., Manchester, VT.
The Park-McCullough House, North Bennington, VT.

Library of Congress Cataloging-in-Publication Data
Harris, Bill, 1933-
        Historic homes of New England.
                p.   cm.
        ISBN 0-517-47811-0
        1.   Dwellings–New England–Pictorial works.   2. New England–
        –Description and travel–1981-   –Views.   3.   Historic buildings–New
        England–Pictorial works.   I. Title.
        F5.H374   1989
        974–dc19   88-37502
                                                                         CIP

CLB 2159
© 1989 Colour Library Books Ltd., Guildford, Surrey, England.
This 1989 edition published by Crescent Books
distributed by Crown Publishers, Inc., 225 Park Avenue South, New York, New York 10003.
Printed and bound in Hong Kong.
ISBN 0 517 47811 0
h g f e d c b a

HISTORIC HOMES
of
NEW ENGLAND

Text by
BILL HARRIS

Photography by
RIC PATTISON

CRESCENT BOOKS
NEW YORK

When Americans dream of New England, as they often do, the dream sometimes revolves around Cape Cod cottages with rose-covered picket fences or saltbox farmhouses with walk-in fireplaces.

Call it quaint, call it cute, call it a part of the American heritage, but there was a time in our recent history when novelist Edith Wharton wrote off those typical New England homes as places where tight-lipped women with thin hair gathered at the napes of their necks sat around wearing shawls and wire-rimmed spectacles, earnestly eating blueberry pie. A half-century before Mrs. Wharton dismissed the New England tradition, an 1848 architectural guide was almost joyful in pointing out that the original builders of colonial structures had used "perishable materials," with the result that their creations wouldn't last much longer and travelers soon wouldn't have to put up with them. Then the great architect Richard Upjohn stepped into the controversy in the 1870s and told his followers that the laws of harmony were taken much more seriously by those earlier builders and their work deserved a second look. The message was taken to heart by architects who mattered, and colonial buildings became fashionable again. The originals didn't turn out to be as perishable as predicted, and the imitations produced by the Colonial Revival movement of a century ago are part and parcel of what we consider New England's charm today.

But there is more to New England than colonial charm. Every architectural fashion that has ever touched America has touched the six New England states, often starting there, always flourishing there. The mix is as fascinating as American culture itself. The Romanesque style of H.H. Richardson complements the Georgian style of Charles Bulfinch and both exist as naturally among Victorian mansions and covered bridges in the same way as the Beaux Arts homes of Newport serve as a chapter in the adventure of exploring the cottages of Cape Cod.

The original New Englanders who arrived at Cape Cod in 1620 weren't too interested in building impressive houses. The Bible told them that mansions had been prepared for the faithful in Heaven, and that was good enough for them. In the meantime, the Pilgrims were content with whatever providence might send their way. A contemporary visitor reported that "they burrow themselves in the earth." He described their first houses as hillsides timbered over and covered with dirt. The rain came in and the smoke from their fires couldn't get out, but it was home and it was only temporary. Within a few years, most were living in wood-frame houses patterned after the ones they had left behind in the south of England. A few, praise God, were even made of brick.

The rewards of Heaven notwithstanding, the Puritans who settled the Bay Colony a few years later brought the idea of personal profit along with them. And as the upper class prospered, the merchants began reasoning that God probably wouldn't be offended if they built fine houses for themselves. As long as they provided a prominent church and a comfortable home for its minister, they told themselves that God would probably even be pleased if His house was in an up-scale neighborhood. And their earthly mansions would provide His less ambitious servants with an incentive to work harder to produce more for themselves and the common good.

But even before their colonies were a generation old, they were faced with a problem of tradition. Assigned building lots were too narrow for anything that could be considered truly grand, and a man was well-advised not to be too ostentatious or the message would be misconstrued. In the southern colonies, merchants and planters added side wings to their homes as their affluence increased. But the New England pattern forced them to find their extra space in wings added to the back. It made the houses roomier and more comfortable, but didn't impress anybody except the people who lived in them. And what's the point of having a fine house if the neighbors don't notice? One way of solving the problem was to expand upward and create a three-story house among the simple cottages. When they did, the neighbors not only took notice, but they were forced to look up to their betters. It was a wonderful solution to the social problem, but a headache for builders. Their basic design was nothing more or less than a wooden box, and extending it upward only emphasized the boxiness. They found relief in cornices and rooftop balustrades, and usually made the third-floor windows smaller to de-emphasize the height. They also began adding front porches, elaborate doorways and Palladian windows and, by the 19th century, most of the problems had been solved. Most three-story New England houses still had all the characteristics of a box, but the devices that hid the fact gave them a character all their own.

As families moved away from the Bay Colony into the Connecticut River Valley and other wide-open places, they didn't take advantage of the space to spread their houses out rather than up. The square design was easier to heat, a very important consideration, but it was also felt to be safer to stick with what the Establishment back in Boston considered elegant than to break new ground. Most of the builders were carpenters rather than architects and probably didn't have the resources to create new statements. Until the 18th century, they relied on English-produced carpenter's handbooks, adapting the ideas to their own terrain. Their houses were plain, simple and practical. The rooms were small and low, easy to build and easy to heat. There were rarely more than four rooms, divided equally between two floors and around a central fireplace. Almost no thought was given to decoration, although the early builders discovered that pine, the most common building material, was much easier to carve than the oak that was used in English houses, and many gave in to the temptation to give their work a stamp of individuality. But their creations were basically as alike as modern tract houses, and their designs were just as comfortable in town as in the countryside. When New England produced its first professional architect, his inspiration came from townhouses rather than sprawling country estates. His influence extended to other designer-builders and created the great Federal Era that lasted from the 1780s through the 1830s. His name was Charles Bulfinch. His monument is the State House in Boston and his legacy is all over New England. Yet his original plan was to become a merchant.

After graduating from Harvard, Bulfinch took a Grand Tour of Europe where he visited all the great cities, from Florence to London. When he was in Paris, he met Thomas Jefferson, a well-known amateur architect, and was as impressed by what the Virginian had to tell him about art and architecture as by the man himself. When he got back to Boston, a miserable failure in a shipping scheme landed him in debtors' prison and forced him to abandon his plan to become a merchant prince. As soon as his financial health improved, he began dabbling in real estate. He filled one large parcel of land with a series of row houses patterned after the work of Robert Adam, which he had studied in Edinburgh. They were beautiful, but he couldn't sell them and he was forced to declare bankruptcy. He tried again with a similar development along the Charles River, but lost his shirt a second time. It was not for nothing that he advised a relative interested in becoming an architect that no young man could make a living that way. On the other hand, he hadn't been able to make a living in the shipping business, either. But he managed to get enough architectural commissions to keep body and soul together at least. In the process, he helped New England discover its own architectural soul.

Winds of change began blowing into New England from New York and Philadelphia during the years before the Civil War when fashion decreed that the country should be remade in the Gothic style. The earlier passion for Federal houses had already given way to a similar Greek Revival, and set the stage for what builders and interior designers began hailing as romance. The very word "Gothic" gave them images of castles and cathedrals to sell, and what could be more romantic than that? It was considered the height of elegance at mid-century and, when the Wadsworth Atheneum was built in Hartford in 1842, the rush began in earnest to build mansions with arched windows, elaborate traceries, castellated towers and dark, cluttered interiors.

The spirit of romance continued through the post-Civil War years, but the war itself produced hundreds of new millionaires, all anxious to make sure their neighbors were aware of their presence. Living in an adaptation of a medieval castle was just fine, but a real statement called for new ideas. Their architects obliged with an updated version of the Gothic, as interpreted by John Ruskin's writings on Venice, and offered them an alternative choice with the introduction of Second Empire France and its proliferation of mansard roofs to the New England countryside. The polychromed bricks of Venetian-Gothic villas made good neighbors for houses of native red brick, and windows set into the mansards were only a few steps removed from the traditional dormers of the Colonial Revival houses.

The nouveaux riches of the late nineteenth century brought a flamboyance to New England that would have shocked the Founding Fathers. Many of their descendants in Boston breathed a quiet sigh of relief in 1872 when Henry Hobson Richardson won the commission to design

Boston's Trinity Church. Some Bostonians were suspicious of him because he was a Southerner from Louisiana. But it was to his credit that he hadn't fought in the recent war, and his credentials were further enhanced by the fact that he was a Harvard man. Better still, he had designed two new buildings for the university, which made him the next best thing to a local boy. But even purists who considered Richardson an out-of-towner agreed his Trinity Church was the statement they were all waiting for Boston to make. It had the vitality that had become so important, but it also had the qualities all New England was longing for: order and restraint.

It was the beginning of a new architectural age that lasted well into the twentieth century. The Trinity commission brought a rush of new business to Richardson's office, from influential Episcopalians and Harvard men alike. One of the most important of his new jobs was an assignment to design all the public buildings for the town of North Easton, Massachusetts, as well as a mansion for its leading citizen, Frederick Ames (Harvard '54). The mansion was never built, but the other buildings, especially the railroad station, led to an assignment to design the suburban stations of the Boston & Albany Railroad. Richardson designed public buildings and private homes all over New England and up and down the Eastern Seaboard after that. And after the Chicago fire, he changed the face of that city, too. His work there gave him a national reputation and he began transforming the look of cities all the way to the West Coast. In the process, with the style known as Richardson Romanesque, he became the only architect in American history to have an architectural movement named for him. But it wasn't his only gift to the look of America. His development of the so-called Shingle style, a direct descendant of the popular Queen Anne houses, brought New England architecture full-circle, back to its Colonial beginnings.

As Richardson was bringing restrained good taste back to New England, exuberance was the word of the day down in its southeast corner. Restraint was hardly what anyone had in mind during Newport's Gilded Age, and whether or not they had even good taste in mind is still a matter for the eye of the beholder. But what a beauty it is to behold. No one would ever consider the mansions of Newport typically "New England," but they aren't "typical" of anything else, either.

New England historians usually write off Newport as a creation of New Yorkers, and it's true that most of the elaborate mansions were designed by New York architects for New York millionaires. But the trend was started by summer visitors from the South who discovered the place in 1784.

It was nearly a century before New York society arrived, led by Caroline Schermerhorn Astor. She had been influenced by Ward McAllister, a Georgian who had discovered a talent for cultivating the rich and successful during summer sojourns at Newport. After taking charge of Caroline Astor's social life, it was only natural that he should lure her to his favorite summer place, and just as natural that her social set would follow them.

He helped her find a marble palace worthy of her station in life and, even before she moved in, her brother-in-law, John Jacob Astor III, began building a reproduction of a French chateau a stone's-throw away. They were to form a beachhead that promised to keep Newport society as rigidly structured as New York's. And Mrs. Astor was determined to make sure that the likes of the Harrimans and Goulds, J.P. Morgan and John D. Rockefeller stayed away. She paid the bills for most of the lavish parties that kept Newport summers humming, and that allowed her to determine the strict order of the daily carriage parades on Bellevue Avenue, to keep the unwashed from bathing at Bailey's Beach and to monitor the membership of important local clubs. She worked hard in her role as social arbiter and no one thought of challenging her role as queen.

Among the families she was determined to keep away were the descendants of Cornelius Vanderbilt. Their fortune was well over $100 million, and they had built a string of lavish mansions on New York's Fifth Avenue, but even members of the family's third generation went to work every day on a railroad, of all things. It simply didn't fit Caroline's idea of what was socially acceptable.

But when Alva Smith of Mobile, Alabama, married Willie K. Vanderbilt, the old Commodore's grandson, she decided to give Caroline a run for her money and succeeded, in New York, by giving the most lavish party the city had ever seen. After Caroline and her daughter had special dresses made for it, they discovered they hadn't been invited. When asked why, Alva said she didn't know anyone named Astor. None had ever called at her house, and none had ever invited her to any of their parties. The oversight was corrected and, in 1892, Willie felt free to invade the Astor colony by giving Alva a new house in Newport as a birthday present. He had been impressed by the monumental Gothic Ochre Court, designed for real-estate millionaire Ogden Goelet by Richard Morris Hunt, and commissioned Hunt to build him something better. Marble House cost the Vanderbilt heir nine million dollars to build and another two million to furnish. Novelist Henry James called it a "white elephant," but he didn't turn down invitations to parties there. And it didn't deter Willie's brother, Cornelius II, from hiring Hunt to build him a rival palace, The Breakers, for his wife, the former Alice Gwynn.

Cornelius and Alice had arrived in Newport before his brother and settled down in a mansion he bought from tobacco millionaire, Pierre Lorillard. The original house burned to the ground, which Vanderbilt must have considered a golden opportunity. When he was told of the fire, he said, "I don't care so much about the house, it can be rebuilt." It was and, if Alva felt upstaged, she didn't say so. She divorced Willie a month before her former brother-in-law moved into his new house and settled for nothing more than a $100,000-a-year income, custody of their three children and the deed to Marble House.

The summer people at Newport always referred to their houses as "cottages," and visitors there today usually smirk at the idea. But what they aren't told by the tour guides, and probably wouldn't believe anyway, is that the Astors, the Vanderbilts and the others had a sense of humor. They knew very well what they had created and thought that calling them cottages added just the right casual touch. When Alva got her divorce, she had proof that her former husband had taken up with Nellie Neustader, the wife of a San Francisco cigar salesman. With evidence like that, he would surely have given her their Fifth Avenue mansion in New York if she had asked for it. That house had also been designed by Richard Morris Hunt and, of all his work, it was the architect's personal favorite. His fellow architect, Charles McKim, said that walking past it always made him sleep better. But in the end, Alva Vanderbilt chose the house in New England as the place she preferred to sleep.

The old Vanderbilt mansion in New York has long since been demolished. But Marble House, The Breakers and most of their Newport neighbors are still standing and still dazzling visitors. Purists may not consider them part of the New England tradition, but the fact they have been preserved is very much a part of it. The past is alive and well and living all over New England.

Visitor's Guide

Most of the homes pictured in these pages may be visited.

Maine

Hamilton House, Vaughn's Lane, South Berwick, Maine 03908 (207-384-5269) (pp.11-14). Open June 1 to October 15, Tuesday, Thursday, Saturday and Sunday, noon–5p.m. Its garden is also available for weddings and special events. Admission charged.*

Sayward-Wheeler House, 79 Barrell Lane, York Harbor, Maine 03911 (207-384-5269) (pp.15-17). Open June 1 to October 15, Tuesday, Thursday, Saturday and Sunday, noon–5p.m. Admission charged.*

New Hampshire

Moffatt-Ladd House and Garden, 154 Market Street, Portsmouth, New Hampshire 03801 (603-436-821) (pp.18-21). Open daily June 15 to October 15, 10a.m.–4p.m., Sunday 2p.m.–5p.m. Admission charged.

Wentworth-Coolidge Mansion, Little Harbor Road, off Route 1A, Portsmouth, New Hampshire 03801 (603-436-6607) (pp.22,23). Open late May to mid-June on weekends; mid-June to Labor Day, daily. Admission charged.

Barrett House, Main Street, New Ipswich, New Hampshire 03071 (617-227-3956) (p.27). Open June 1 to October 15, Tuesday through Sunday, noon–5p.m. Admission charged.*

Franklin Pierce Homestead, Routes 9 and 31, Hillsboro, New Hampshire 03244 (603-478-3165) (pp.28,29). Open weekends late May, June and September; July, August and October, Friday, Saturday and Sunday. Admission charged.

Governor John Langdon Mansion, 143 Pleasant Street, Portsmouth, New Hampshire 03801 (603-436-3205) (pp.30-33). Open June 1 to October 15, Wednesday through Sunday. The gardens may be rented for weddings and parties. Admission charged.*

Vermont

Hildene, Manchester Village, Vermont 05254 (802-362-1788) (pp.34-39). Open mid-May to late October. In the winter months, the estate is used for cross-country skiing. Admission charged.

Park-McCullough House, West Street, North Bennington, Vermont 05257 (802-442-5441) (pp.40-43). Open daily late May to October. Admission fee includes historic slide show. Horse-drawn sleigh rides, candlelight tours and special exhibitions are scheduled regularly.

Calvin Coolidge Homestead, Plymouth Notch, Vermont 05056 (802-828-3226) (pp.46,47). Open daily mid-May to late October. Admission charged. The Historic District also includes a Carpenter Gothic church, a 19th-century barn with farm implements and a museum with a restaurant. It is near a 16,000-acre state forest.

Massachusetts

Colonel Josiah Quincy House, 20 Muirhead Street, Wollaston, Massachusetts 02170 (617-227-3956) (pp.48,49). Open June 1 to October 15, noon–5p.m. Admission charged.*

Beauport, Sleeper-McCann House, 75 Eastern Point Boulevard, Gloucester, Massachusetts 01930 (508-283-0800) (pp.50-53). Open mid-May through mid-October, Monday through Friday, 10a.m.–4p.m. Admission charged.*

Hammond Castle Museum, 80 Hesperus Avenue, Gloucester, Massachusetts 01930 (508-283-0800) (pp.54,55). Open daily. Admission fee includes a guided tour. The castle also has a rooftop cafe, and demonstrations of the organ can be arranged.

Sargent House, 49 Middle Street, Gloucester, Massachusetts 01930 (508-281-2432) (pp.56,57). Open June to September, Tuesday, Thursday and Saturday, or by appointment. Admission charged.

Gore Place, 52 Gore Street, Waltham, Massachusetts 02154 (617-894-2798) (pp.58-63). Open April 15 to November 15, Tuesday through Saturday 10a.m.–5p.m.; Sunday 2p.m.–5p.m. Admission fee includes a guided tour. The grounds are open year 'round during daylight hours.

Ropes Mansion and Garden, 318 Essex Street, Salem, Massachusetts 01970 (617-744-0718) (pp.64-66). Open June 1 to October 31, except Mondays. Admission charge for the Mansion includes a guided tour. The garden, also available for weddings and parties, is open without charge during the growing season, except Sundays.

Codman House, The Grange, Codman Road, Lincoln, Massachusetts 01773. (617-259-8843) (pp.68-71). Open June 1 to October 15, Wednesday through Sunday. Admission charge includes guided tours at noon and 1p.m. The garden is available for weddings and parties.*

The Adams National Historic Site, Peacefield, 135 Adams Street, Quincy, Massachusetts 02169 (617-773-1177) (pp.72-75). Open daily mid-April to mid-November. Admission charged. The John and John Quincy Adams birthplaces, two 17th-century saltbox houses, are also part of the Historic Site.

The John Fitzgerald Kennedy National Historic Site, 83 Beals Street, Brookline, Massachusetts 02146 (617-566-7937) (pp.76-79). Open daily. Admission charged.

Connecticut

Webb-Deane-Stevens Museum, 211 Main Street, Wethersfield, Connecticut 06109 (203-529-0612) (pp.80-83). A complex of three houses, including the Joesph Webb and Silas Deane Houses. Open Tuesday through Saturday 10a.m.–4p.m.; Sunday 1p.m.–4p.m. (extended hours May 15 to October 15). Admission charge includes a guided tour.

Bowen House, Roseland Cottage, Route 169, Woodstock, Connecticut 06281 (203-928-4074) (pp.84-87). Open May 25 to September 18, Wednesday through Sunday; September 23 to October 16, Friday through Sunday, noon to 5p.m. Admission charged.*

The Harriet Beecher Stowe House, 73 Forest Street, Hartford, Connecticut 06105 (203-525-9317) (pp.88,89). Open daily June through October and in December; closed Mondays other months. Admission fee also includes the nearby **Mark Twain House** (pp.90-95) which is open on the same schedule.

Gillette Castle, Hadlyme, Connecticut 06423 (203-526-2336) (pp.98-103). Open daily late May to mid-October and on weekends through December. Admission is charged for the castle, but the state park surrounding it is free.

Lockwood-Mathews Mansion, 295 West Avenue, Norwalk, Connecticut 06850. (203-838-1434) (pp.104-107). Open Tuesday through Friday 11a.m–4p.m.; Sunday 1p.m.–4p.m. Admission fee includes a guided tour.

Rhode Island

Gilbert Stuart Birthplace, Saunderstown, Rhode Island 02874 (401-294-3001) (pp.108-111). Open April 1 to November 15, 11a.m–5p.m., closed Fridays. Admission charged.

Blithewold Gardens and Arboretum, 101 Ferry Road, Bristol, Rhode Island 02809 (401-253-2707) (pp.116,117). The grounds are open all year, and the mansion from May through October, except Mondays and holidays. There are separate admission charges for the grounds and the mansion.

Beechwood, Bellevue Avenue, Newport, Rhode Island 02840 (401-846-3772) (p.119). Open all year with varying seasonal hours. A theatrical tour is staged from June through October, with actors portraying Mrs. Astor's servants and guests. Admission charged.

Wanton-Lyman-Hazard House, 17 Broadway, Newport, Rhode Island 02840 (401-846-0813) (p.119). Open June through August, Tuesday through Saturday. Admission charged.

The Breakers, Ochre Point Avenue, Newport, Rhode Island 02840 (401-847-1000) (pp.122,123). Open daily, April through October. Admission charged.

The Elms, Bellevue Avenue, Newport, Rhode Island 02840 (401-847-1000) (pp.124-135). Open daily, April through October; weekends, November through March. Admission charged.

Rosecliff, Bellevue Avenue, Newport, Rhode Island 02840 (401-847-1000) (pp.136-141). Open daily, April through October. Admission charged.

Château-Sur-Mer, Bellevue Avenue, Newport, Rhode Island 02840 (401-847-1000) (pp.142-147). Open daily, May through October; weekends, November through April. Admission charged.

Marble House, Bellevue Avenue, Newport, Rhode Island 02840 (401-847-1000) (pp.148-160). Open daily, April through October; weekends, November through March. Admission charged.

The Preservation Society of Newport County, (401-847-1000), provides information and sells combination admission tickets to the buildings it administers, including The Elms, The Breakers, Rosecliff, Marble House, Château-Sur-Mer, Hunter House and Kingscote.

* These houses are properties of the Society for the Preservation of New England Antiquities, which maintains thirty-four properties all over New England. For membership information, write to the SPNEA at 141 Cambridge Street, Boston, Massachusetts, or call (617) 227-3956.

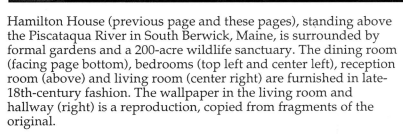

Hamilton House (previous page and these pages), standing above the Piscataqua River in South Berwick, Maine, is surrounded by formal gardens and a 200-acre wildlife sanctuary. The dining room (facing page bottom), bedrooms (top left and center left), reception room (above) and living room (center right) are furnished in late-18th-century fashion. The wallpaper in the living room and hallway (right) is a reproduction, copied from fragments of the original.

Hamilton House, built in 1785, was restored by Emily Tyson and her stepdaughter, Mrs. Henry Vaughan, in 1898. They created the imposing formal gardens (this page), setting trellises and statuary among stately flower beds and making pathways through the nearby woods, which are now part of a state park. The Sayward-Wheeler House (facing page top and overleaf) in York Harbor, Maine, a unique example of solid New England vernacular style, has stood virtually unaltered since it was built in 1720. Its main entrance originally faced a wharf on the York River (facing page bottom and overleaf), which was useful to its first owner, Jonathan Sayward, who was a merchant and shipowner.

The Moffatt-Ladd House (these pages) in Portsmouth, New Hampshire, was built in 1763 as a wedding gift to Samuel and Sarah Moffatt by the bridegroom's father, John Moffatt. Its entrance hall and the elaborately carved staircase (top left and top) take up a third of the ground floor. The fireplace in the dining room (above and left) is surrounded by English tiles, and the pantry conceals a secret entrance to the wine cellar.

The Ship Room (right) of the Moffatt-Ladd House (these pages), Portsmouth, New Hampshire, overlooked the wharves of the Moffatt family, some of whose portraits still hang in the house (below right). William Whipple, a signatory of the Declaration of Independence, later lived here. The Yellow Chamber (below) is named for the color of its damask curtains and upholstery; whereas the President's Room (bottom) was furnished by former presidents of the Society of Colonial Dames, which owns the Moffatt-Ladd House. The back parlor (facing page top) is dominated by a magnificent mahogany breakfront cabinet, and the kitchen (facing page bottom) by imposing, built-in cabinets.

One of the few Colonial governors' homes to survive unchanged, the Wentworth-Coolidge Mansion (these pages) in Portsmouth, New Hampshire, was built for Benning Wentworth, Royal Governor from 1741 to 1767. It was expanded and restored in 1920 by John T. Coolidge, an artist and antiquarian, and Henry Wadsworth Longfellow wrote of the mansion in *The Poet's Tale*, as "A noble pile,/ Baronial and Colonial in its style,/ Gables and dormer windows everywhere,/ And stacks of chimneys rising high in air."

The 18th-century MacPheadris-Warner House (these pages), often referred to as Warner House, the oldest house in Portsmouth, New Hampshire, was among the first to be designated a National Historic Landmark. It was built for Captain Archibald MacPheadris. The furnishings, some of which are museum pieces on loan, and the clothing, neatly hung (above), give the impression of a house whose owners have just stepped away for a few minutes. The murals in the stairway (right) are thought to be the oldest still in place in the United States. They represent two of the five Indian sachems who visited London with Peter Schuyler in 1710. The visit was painted by Verelst and many mezzotints of his pictures were later produced. The MacPheadris-Warner murals are thought to be a copy of such a mezzotint.

The fireplace in the dining room (facing page) of the MacPheadris-Warner House is framed with Dutch sepia tiles depicting scenes from 18th-century light opera. Blackburn portraits, in matching frames, of Jonathan Warner and his wife – the former Mary Macpheadris, daughter of Captain Archibald MacPheadris, who built the house – grace the walls of the dining room. Barrett House (this page), Forest Hall in New Ipswich, New Hampshire, was built in 1800 by mill owner Charles Barrett for his son, in response to a challenge from the young man's father-in-law, who promised to furnish any house he could build in as grand a manner as he could build it. The challenge was met with this stately, three-story Federal mansion. The present furnishings, as elegant as the house itself, were accumulated over the following hundred years by later generations of the Barrett family. The house itself is sited on a terrace, surrounded by a hundred acres of woods and meadows.

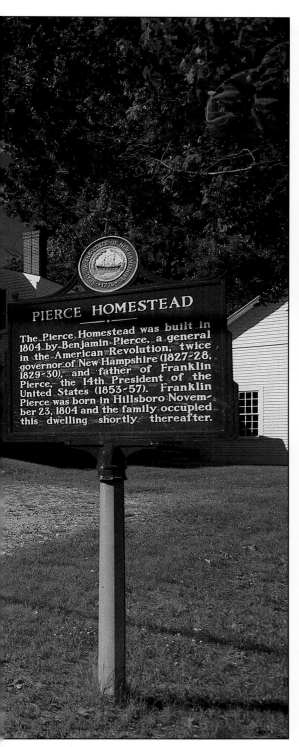

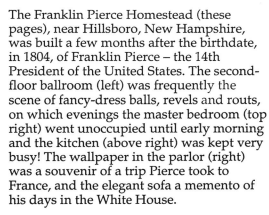

The Franklin Pierce Homestead (these pages), near Hillsboro, New Hampshire, was built a few months after the birthdate, in 1804, of Franklin Pierce – the 14th President of the United States. The second-floor ballroom (left) was frequently the scene of fancy-dress balls, revels and routs, on which evenings the master bedroom (top right) went unoccupied until early morning and the kitchen (above right) was kept very busy! The wallpaper in the parlor (right) was a souvenir of a trip Pierce took to France, and the elegant sofa a memento of his days in the White House.

The Governor John Langdon Mansion Memorial (these pages) in Portsmouth, New Hampshire, was, of all the houses in the city, George Washington's favorite. Its interior is as richly-ornamented as its Georgian facade, and is furnished with pieces which were very fashionable in 1789, when it was built. The Colonial Revival dining room (facing page bottom right) was built in 1906 to a design by Stanford White, who also effected minor alterations to the front portico. The dining room was inspired by an oval room in an older house now preserved as part of Portsmouth's Rockingham Hotel.

These pages: the striking, carved rococo ornamentation of the interior of Langdon Mansion. Joiners Daniel Hart and Michael Whidden III created elegant patterns commissioned by John Langdon, whose portrait hangs in the parlor (facing page top).

Hildene (these pages) – "hill and valley" – in Manchester Village, Vermont, was the summer retreat of Robert Todd Lincoln, eldest son of Abraham and Mary Todd Lincoln. He bought the house in 1902, and the Lincoln family were to live there up until 1975. The house's library (facing page top) once held his father's papers. The late-Victorian parlor furnishings (facing page bottom) are from the Iowa home of his father-in-law, Senator James Harlan.

Hildene's spacious, bright front hall (left) and Grand Staircase (above left) are a welcoming beginning to a tour of the house (these pages). The walls of the Queen Anne-furnished dining room (above and below) are half covered in wooden paneling and edged with a dado rail, which gives them a solid, three-dimensional effect enhanced by the wall paintings. The formal gardens (facing page and overleaf) are set against the Green and Taconic mountains, overlooking the Battenkill Valley.

The Park-McCullough House (these pages), an 1865, Second Empire, Victorian mansion in North Bennington, Vermont, was designed by architects Diaper and Dudley. It was once the scene of an endless round of parties, planned in the Ladies' Morning Room (left) and staged in the dining room (facing page top), which could seat as many as eighteen guests. After dinner, the women withdrew to the Ladies' Parlor (facing page bottom) while the men retired to the Governor's Study (overleaf) for a cigar and talk of politics. The room was named for Governor John McCullough, the first of two Vermont governors to live in the mansion.

The 1851 Justin Smith Morrill Homestead (these pages) in Strafford, Vermont, is a Gothic Revival masterpiece, built for the U.S. representative and senator, Justin Morrill, who pioneered legislation to provide the states with land and federal funds for the endowment of agricultural and technical colleges.

He gave his name to the 1862 and 1890 Morrill Acts. The house is noted for its intricate turrets, balconies and dormers. The second-floor, hooded French windows were later additions that give just the right complement to the elaborate pendants and other decorative elements of the exterior.

Calvin Coolidge took the Presidential oath of office to become the country's thirtieth president on August 3rd, 1923, using the Bible still on the desk in the former dining room (right) of his family homestead (these pages) in Plymouth Notch, Vermont. When the oath-taking was over, he went upstairs to bed (above right), and the next day had breakfast in the kitchen (above and top right) as though nothing had happened. He often returned to the homestead for vacations after he left the White House, having refused renomination in 1928, to sit on the porch and count the cars driving past for a look at the presidential birthplace.

The 1770 Colonel Josiah Quincy House (these pages) in Wollaston, Massachusetts, is a Georgian classic, designed and furnished by the Colonel himself. Its exterior includes an interesting combination of a Chinese-style fretwork balustrade and a classical portico. The parlors (left and facing page top) retain their original moldings along with furniture that has been in the Quincy family for 250 years. The Liverpool tiles around the dining room fireplace (facing page bottom) were imported from England by the Colonel, a leader of the American Revolution, when the house was built. Initially, the house had an unobstructed view of Boston across the bay. The view and surroundings of the house have, of course, changed now, but the house has remained the same.

Built over a period of twenty-seven years by the collector Henry Davis Sleeper, Beauport (these pages), in Gloucester, Massachusetts, contains some forty rooms full of decorative objects and paneling from old New England houses. Sleeper was among the first to appreciate folk art and pine furniture, and the house was a very influential recreation of Colonial America. Beauport is perched on rocks with a dramatic view overlooking Gloucester Harbor. Such nautical influences are reflected in the Golden Step Room (facing page top), which contains a model of the ship that is its namesake. The Octagon Room (facing page bottom) is a splendid tribute to French-American friendship, and in the library (above) hangs an original Pine Tree flag – the ancestor of Old Glory. The Benjamin Franklin Room (above right) is one of several tributes to men whom Henry Sleeper admired. The China Trade Room (overleaf), so-called because it is hung with 18th-century wallpaper made in Canton, was later refurnished as a Chippendale parlor by subsequent owner, Charles McCann. The house is, officially, known as Beauport, Sleeper-McCann House.

"It is a marvelous thing, this expression of human ideals in walls and windows," wrote inventor John Hays Hammond, Jr. in 1929. His romantic castle, Hammond Castle (these pages), overlooking the Port of Gloucester, Massachusetts, contains his impressive collection of Roman, medieval and Renaissance artifacts. The house is full of strange and wonderful things – for example, the one-hundred-foot-long Great Hall (right), with its eighty-five-foot-high tower, can easily accommodate the largest pipe organ ever built for a private home – 8,200 pipes in all, and the courtyard's plants (facing page bottom) are kept fresh with artificial rainstorms. Hammond was America's second greatest inventor – next to Thomas Edison – producing over 100 patents. He conducted his famous experiments in radio remote-control with boats in the port below his house.

The Sargent House (these pages), a late-18th-century Georgian structure in Gloucester, Massachusetts, contains outstanding examples of period furniture and artifacts in its parlors (below and left), dining room (bottom) and bedrooms, including a drawing room chair from the palace of Marie Antoinette. Among its residents was John Murray, founder of the Universalist Church in America.

Gore Place (these pages), in Waltham, Massachusetts, the great Federal estate of former governor and U.S. senator, Christopher Gore, was built in 1806 to plans by the prominent French architect Jacques Guillaume Legrand. It was built over the site of the former Gore residence, which was destroyed by fire. The rooms on the first floor: the Oval Salon (above left), the parlor (above right and facing page top) and the small dining room

(facing page bottom), are distinguished by unusual curved wall surfaces. Paintings hanging in the house include a portrait of Gore by John Trumball and one of his daughter by Christopher Copley, both the work of personal friends. His attentive interest in students ensured that these elegant surroundings were often filled with students visiting him from Harvard.

The dramatic, circular stairway (above) at Gore Place (these pages) rises fifteen and a half feet above the marble-paved main entrance hall. The portrait on the wall at the top of the stairs is of Rebecca Payne Gore, Christopher Gore's wife, who commissioned Legrand and worked closely with him on the design of the mansion. More than twenty period rooms are preserved in the house. Each, including the bedchambers (facing page), is a tribute to Mrs. Gore's fine taste and sense of style. She created what was called "the finest mansion in New England."

The French-Empire chandelier in the entrance hall (facing page top) of Gore Place (these pages) once belonged to Daniel Webster, who read law under Christopher Gore. The billiard table (right) in the billiard room was owned by Christopher Gore, and was later used by the families of Theodore Lyman Jr., Charles Metz, Theophilus Walker and others who lived here and relaxed in the Family Parlor (facing page bottom).

The interior of the Colonial Ropes Mansion (these pages) in Salem, Massachusetts, was renovated in the 19th century, but the exterior retained its original character. It has recently been refurbished with reproductions of 1890s wallcoverings and carpets in the parlor (left), Eliza Ropes's bedroom (facing page top) and the dining room (facing page bottom).

The master bedroom (facing page top) and the sitting room (facing page bottom) reflect the daily lives of the descendants of Judge Nathaniel Ropes, whose family lived in the Ropes Mansion for four generations. The Peirce-Nichols House (this page), also in Salem, an outstanding combination of Georgian and Adamesque styles, was the home of successive generations of two families dating back to the 1780s, when it was built by a prominent local merchant, Jerethmiel Peirce. Both mansions, along with others nearby, have survived intact into our own time as reminders of daily life in Salem a century ago.

The Codman House (these pages) in Lincoln, Massachusetts, was inherited by the merchant, John Codman, who expanded and renovated it in the style of architect Charles Bulfinch. At the turn of the century his descendant, the noted interior designer, Ogden Codman Jr., restored many of the rooms and added the elegant Italianate garden. In 1863, John Hubbard Sturgis converted the back parlor into an Elizabethan Revival dining room (facing page bottom), using rich colors and butternut wood. The upstairs central hall and staircase (above right) was inspired by the John Hancock house in Boston. The library (top and above left) was decorated by Ogden Codman, Jr.

The front parlor (facing page top) is the centerpiece of the Codman House (these pages). But the room behind it, often called the ballroom (top) is equally dramatic. The main bedrooms (above and facing page bottom) are arranged around the central stairway, while the guest rooms (right and above right) are in a wing above the servants' quarters and kitchen.

When future President John Adams bought the house he later called "Peacefield" (these pages) in 1788 it had been a Quincy, Massachusetts, landmark for fifty years. He died nearly forty years later in the study (above) which his wife, Abigail, an indefatigable home improver, had had built for him. His son, President John Quincy Adams, also lived in the house, sometimes known as Adams Mansion, as did four further generations of the family. The stone library (facing page bottom) was built by Charles Francis Adams to house the presidential papers of his father and grandfather.

The library (facing page bottom) of Peacefield (these pages) was the focus of Charles Francis Adams's life for more than four decades while he catalogued the chronicles of one of New England's most important families. The other rooms in the house, including his grandfather's study (above) and the master bedroom (facing page top), contain their original furnishings, and memories of two presidents.

On May 29th, 1917, President John F. Kennedy was born in this house, now the John Fitzgerald Kennedy National Historic Site (these pages) in Brookline, Massachusetts. The coal stove in the kitchen (left) often produced cookies and other treats to sustain the singers gathered around the piano during family singing sessions in the living room (below). J.F.K's cigar box and the family photograph, both on top of the piano, are among dozens of mementoes of the president in all parts of the house.

In a corner of the Kennedy dining room (below and bottom), a silver bowl (below), used by Jack Kennedy when he was a baby, can still be seen. The future president was born in his parents' bedroom (facing page top) and took his first trips out into the world in a wicker carriage (facing page bottom) now in the nursery of their Brookline, Massachusetts, home (these pages).

The Silas Deane House (these pages) at Wethersfield, Connecticut, is a restoration of the 1766 home of Silas Deane, a member of the First Continental Congress and the country's first envoy to France. Its bedchambers, parlors, kitchen and other rooms have been furnished with pieces reminiscent of life in the Connecticut River Valley in the 18th century.

The Joseph Webb House (these pages), an impressive neighbor of the Silas Deane House in Wethersfield, was visited by George Washington in 1781. In fact, he slept in one of the bedchambers (above), and met with the French General Rochambeau in the Council Room (top right) to plan the strategy for the Battle of Yorktown. Both the Webb and Deane houses provided models for the architects who initiated the Colonial Revival movement.

Henry C. Bowen's charming Gothic Revival cottage (these pages and overleaf) in Woodstock, Connecticut, is possibly the best-preserved house of its kind in America. A native of Woodstock, Bowen earned his fortune in the dry goods business in New York, where he also published a newspaper.

Back home, he was known for his lavish entertainments, especially his Fourth of July picnics, which brought four American presidents to Woodstock to share the fun. President Grant remembered it fondly after his success in a bowling alley set up in the barn behind the house.

Harriet Beecher Stowe, whose literary output of some thirty volumes includes *Uncle Tom's Cabin,* lived in a house (these pages) in the Hartford, Connecticut, neighborhood known as Nook Farm. Her husband and twin daughters, Harriet and Eliza, shared the comfortable Victorian surroundings, which have been restored after modernization in the 1920s. The rear parlor (facing page top) contains the Stowe's tufted sofa, a violet-patterned china tea set which Mrs. Stowe designed and the Minton Company manufactured, and their replica of the Venus de Milo statue.

"We never came home from an absence that its face did not light up and speak out its eloquent welcome . . . and we could not enter it unmoved," wrote Mark Twain, otherwise known as Samuel L. Clemens, of his house (these pages) in Hartford, Connecticut. Designed in 1873 by Edward Tuckerman Potter and decorated by a group comprising Louis Comfort Tiffany, Lockwood de Forest, Candace Thurber Wheeler and Samuel Coleman, it is a house as happy as anything the writer himself ever created. The neo-Tudor entrance hall and its stairway (right) is, indeed, impressive, as are the elaborate drawing room (facing page top) and dining room (facing page bottom). The schoolroom (overleaf left top) – a former study – was the domain of the children, one of whom, Susy, had her bedroom (overleaf left bottom) nearby. Mrs. Langdon's bedroom (overleaf right top) was set aside for the visits of Mrs. Clemens mother, and was furnished mostly with pieces from her home in Elmira, New York. The bed and dresser in the guest room (overleaf right bottom) are inset with English tiles, which were possibly designed by E. T. Potter for this room.

The billiard room (facing page top) at the top of Mark Twain's house (these pages) was intended as a playroom, but became the author's work place. However, he loved the library (facing page bottom and overleaf) "for its delicious dream of harmonious color and its all-pervading spirit of peace and serenity and deep contentments." The walls of the drawing room (above) are stencilled over with a series of panels featuring East Indian designs in silver over pink, attributed to de Forest.

William Gillette, a successful turn-of-the-century actor and playwright, built a fanciful, imaginative castle (these pages) on a mountain peak in Hadlyme, Connecticut. It stands on the most southerly of a series of seven picturesque hills known as "The Seven Sisters," so he called it "Seventh Sister." Today it is usually known as Gillette Castle. In the conservatory (above), once the home of Gillette's pet frogs, a waterfall plays among the greenery, and there are forty-seven elaborate oak doors in the castle, including the train door (right), each with a different built-in locking device.

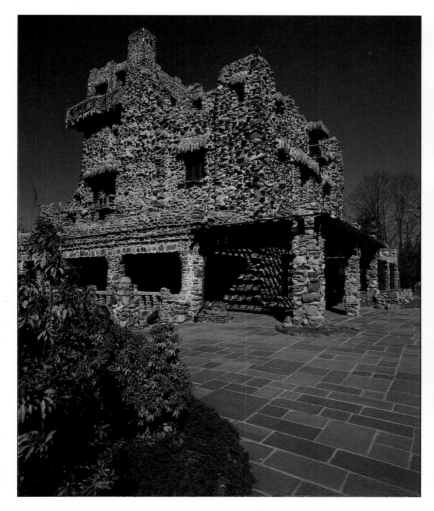

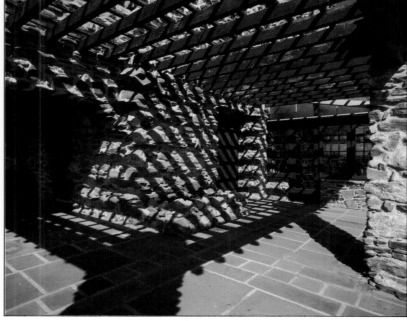

The living room (above and facing page bottom) in Gillette Castle (these pages and overleaf) is fifty feet long and thirty feet wide, with windows reaching all the way up to the nineteen-foot-high ceiling. The grand staircase leads to a balcony, from which the actor intended to stage dramatic entrances – although the room itself probably upstaged him every time. The house is full of imaginative touches: for example, the dining room contains a table that moves along a metal track to accommodate guests. Once locked into place, a touch of one of its panels called the servants from the pantry. The dining room door, like the others (facing page top) in the house, fastens with locks carved from wood. A carpenter worked for a full year to fashion all of them.

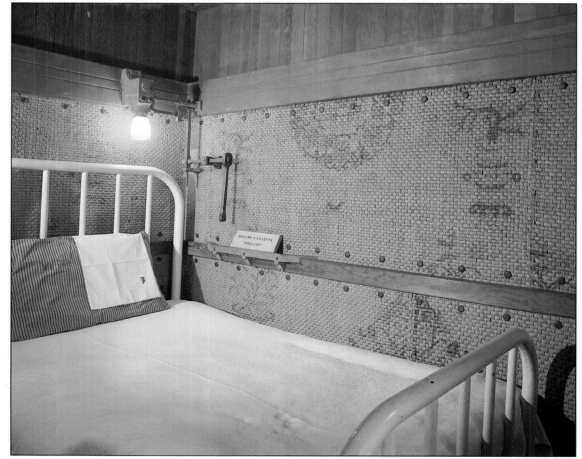

Gillette's study (above), and his
bedroom (left), among the smallest
rooms in the castle, are filled with
built-in gadgetry to make life
pleasanter. His love of nature is
evident in the conservatory (facing
page top). One of the rooms is known
as "Baker Street" (facing page
bottom), honoring Sherlock Holmes,
Gillette's most famous stage role. He
gave the sleuth the image every other
actor has adopted since Gillette's
time.

The high-Victorian Lockwood-Mathews Mansion (these pages) in Norwalk, Connecticut, was built for financier LeGrand Lockwood in 1864. The interior is a feast of carving and painted decoration, with intricate parquet floors and wooden inlays. The music room (facing page bottom) is richly ornamented, but the grand staircase (below and bottom right), rising from a gallery under a skylighted rotunda, is one of the best examples anywhere of the lavish detail that was a hallmark of the era.

Lockwood-Mathews Mansion (these pages) includes many splendid rooms, such as the library (facing page), and the oak paneled French-Renaissance dining room (right). There are also nine bedrooms, most with en-suite dressing rooms, coming off a central balcony (above).

Gilbert Stuart was born in 1755 in a simple room (facing page bottom) in the family homestead (these pages) at Saunderstown, Rhode Island. He was one of America's foremost portrait painters, painting images of presidents Madison, Jefferson, Monroe and Adams. His portrait of George Washington appears on the dollar bill. The faithfully restored gambrel-roofed home is filled with early furniture and tools. Facing page top: the authentically decorated main bedroom.

The snuff mill (above), by which Gilbert Stuart's father used to earn his living, is among the treasures of colonial life, preserved in the Rhode Island house (these pages) where Gilbert Stuart was born. Here, the setting of Stuart's boyhood is faithfully recreated. Each room has a corner fireplace, wide board floors and hand-hewn beams. A grist mill nearby has also been restored and is still turning.

GOVERNOR SPRAGUE
MANSION
Cranston Historical Society

· OPEN FOR TOURS ·
SUNDAYS 2-4 PM · JULY & AUGUST

The homestead (these pages and overleaf) built by William Sprague at Cranston, Rhode Island, in 1790, was home to several generations of one of the first families to operate cotton mills in New England. It was home to two governors, both of whom became U.S. senators, making the mansion an important social center in the 19th century. Its interior is furnished with relics of that era, and its extensive gardens provide a peaceful reminder of that quieter time.

In 1894 when Augustus Van Wickle bought a yacht, he also bought Blithewold, an estate in Bristol, Rhode Island, as a place to moor it. In 1907, his family built a forty-five-room, English-style manor house (these pages) overlooking its arboretum and gardens. Its master bedroom (facing page bottom) also has a sleeping porch (top left), equipped with hammocks, to take advantage of the cool sea breezes during the summers. Other rooms, such as the dining room (center left) are furnished in the style of the late 19th century and are kept filled with fresh flowers from the gardens.

Bristol is one of the showplaces of Rhode Island, holding scores of mansions like the one (above) on Hope Street. But it is often overshadowed by the better known houses in nearby Newport, including Beechwood (facing page top), where Caroline Schermerhorn Astor, *the* Mrs. Astor, reigned over society in the 1890s. The Wanton-Lyman-Hazard House (remaining pictures) in Newport is a memorial of life in 1700. Its parlor (facing page bottom left) was a fashionable gathering place in its day, and morning callers were often shown up to the master bedroom (facing page center left), much as was the custom in Europe.

Newport's Hunter House (these pages) was built in 1748 by the merchant Jonathan Nichols, Jr. When the port fell on hard times after the Revolution, the house was bought by John Hunter, a former U.S. senator. Though named for him, it has been restored to reflect an earlier time. It is most notable for its pine paneling, which is painted to resemble more expensive woods and is particularly fine in the elegant, paneled dining room (below). The house's present furnishings were largely produced by the Townsend and Goddard families, who were considered to be the finest cabinetmakers of Newport's glorious days as a major seaport.

Richard Morris Hunt's Beaux Arts masterpiece, The Breakers (these pages), built for Cornelius Vanderbilt II, is often considered the epitome of Newport. Entire sections of it were built in Europe and reassembled on the site overlooking the sea, a feat that was accomplished in just two years.

Horace Trumbauer, who designed The Elms (these pages), a Newport mansion built for the coal magnate Julius Berwind, never traveled to Europe for inspiration as did other turn-of-the-century architects. However, the classical symmetry of the mansion is nothing if not inspired. Its entrance hall (above) and white marble staircase with wrought iron and bronze railings would have been considered a masterpiece in 18th-century France. Trumbauer was, indeed, something of a Francophile and the entire house would not have been out of place there.

The entrance hall (above and facing page bottom) is an auspicious welcome to The Elms (these pages and overleaf), whose splendor continues unabated through the gallery (facing page top), the ballroom (overleaf left top), the drawing room (overleaf left bottom), the Chinese Breakfast Room (overleaf right top) and the library (overleaf right bottom). The rooms of The Elms were decorated, under the watchful – and profit-oriented – eye of Lord Joseph Duveen by the Paris-based firm of Allard et Fils, later Alavoine et Cie., who scoured France for furniture, paintings and sculpture worthy of Trumbauer's designs for the house.

The dining room (previous pages) of The Elms (these and previous pages) was designed to complement a pair of 18th-century Venetian paintings: the Triumph of Scipio by Paolo Pagani, and Syphax Before Scipio by Giambattista Piazzetta (1706). These were originally part of the decoration in the grand salon at Palazzo Cornaro in Venice. The conservatory (above), a setting for plants and flowers, is, perhaps, the only clue that The

Elms was actually a summer house. The Four Seasons sculptures in the corners of the conservatory were made especially for the room. The walls of Hermione Berwind's bedchamber (facing page bottom) were originally hung with green French silk, as were the windows and bed. Her bathroom (facing page top) has hand-painted porcelain fixtures. After she died in 1922, Mr. Berwind's sister, Julia, occupied these rooms.

The crystal chandelier, furnishings and decorations in the ballroom (facing page bottom left and above) were made especially for The Elms. The room itself, though original, is true to the style of Louis XV. It was little used because Mr. Berwind didn't take vacations and was here only on weekends. When he was in New York, Mrs. Berwind relaxed in her room (facing page top), walked outdoors in the most beautiful garden of any Newport house, or played bridge, sometimes with the servants, in the conservatory, from which she could gaze down the French neoclassical corridors (facing page bottom right) of her elegant home, modeled on the French Château d'Asnières.

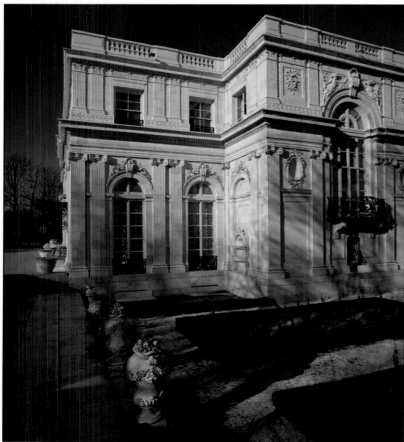

Stanford White recreated Louis XIV's Grand Trianon at Versailles in Rosecliff (these pages), the Newport house he designed for Theresa Fair Oelrichs, whose husband, Hermann, was heir to the North German Lloyd Steamship Line. Her father was one of the "Silver Kings" of Nevada's Comstock Lode. As one of the richest women of her day, Tessie's entertainments in

Rosecliff's ballroom (facing page bottom right) were legendary. The entrance (facing page top), leading to the pale, Caen limestone of the elegantly curved, rococo staircase (facing page bottom left), has an intricate metal tracery over its door and windows, distinguishing them from the other windows of the house.

The ballroom (top and facing page top) of Rosecliff (these pages), forty feet long and eighty feet wide, is the largest in Newport. Its rococo elegance is established by a copy of an 18th-century painting by Jean Antoine Watteau called Fête d'Amour, or Feast of Love, which hangs over the French marble fireplace in the north wall. The dining room (above) and salon (facing page bottom) were designed around rare tapestries, since replaced by damask wall coverings. The elaborate fireplaces in both rooms were made in France.

139

The bedrooms (facing page) at Rosecliff (these pages) are less elegantly decorated than the rooms on the first floor. They are joined to a long corridor (above) through passageways with built-in closets and storage drawers, and most have their own baths. Hermann Oehlrichs, who was not often in residence at Rosecliff, had the billiard room (top) designed to his taste and set off with a carved wooden mantlepiece which he found in Ireland when he and Tessie toured Europe on their wedding trip.

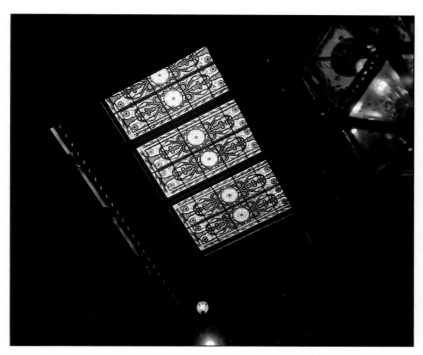

Merchant William Shepard Wetmore commissioned Seth Bradford to build Newport's granite Château-Sur-Mer (these pages) in 1852 as his retirement home. Not content to contemplate the past, he followed up-to-the-minute architectural fashion. By 1871 fashion had changed and Richard Morris Hunt was commissioned to make a silk purse from a Victorian sow's ear. The stairway (this page) is considered by scholars to be Hunt's best work.

The only room Hunt didn't alter at Château-Sur-Mer (these pages) is the ballroom (facing page top), still furnished as it was when the house was built. The drawing room (facing page bottom) was decorated by Ogden Codman, Jr. in 1897. The Turkish Sitting Room (above) is decorated in an Oriental style, fashionable in the 1890s, appropriate when you consider that William Shepard Wetmore, the original owner of the house, had lived in Canton and conducted much business in the Orient. The house, which remained in the Wetmore family until the 1960s, spans an era of gracious Newport living – from before the colony's Gilded Age to well beyond it. It is one of New England's great remaining examples of Victorian architecture.

The bedrooms of Château-Sur-Mer (these pages) used by George Peabody Wetmore (facing page) and his sister, Annie, (top), each contain Renaissance Revival furniture made especially for them. Mr. Wetmore's bedroom has red-stained mahogany paneling made to match the furniture. Château-Sur-Mer's French Salon (above) was created from the original drawing room by Ogden Codman, Jr. while he was collaborating with Edith Wharton on their book, *The Decoration of Houses*.

William K. Vanderbilt commissioned Richard Morris Hunt to design his Newport mansion, Marble House (these pages), to be "the very best living accommodations that money could buy." No one can say he didn't get his money's worth. Hunt based his design on the Petit Trianon at Versailles. The eleven-million-dollar house contains a variety of different kinds of marbles quarried in Europe. Its bronze doors, decorated with the symbol of Louis XIV – a sunburst mask of Apollo – weigh a ton and a half each and turn on pivots rather than hinges. The facade is punctuated with massive Corinthian columns and pilasters.

The two-story entrance hall (these pages) at Marble House, Newport, is lined with yellow Sienna marble and contains two 18th-century Gobelin tapestries. The stair rail and gilded bronze trophies were made in Paris in 1891, according to designs suggested by Mrs. Vanderbilt. The bronze lamp standards and other entrance hall appointments were also made for the house. Most of the furnishings present in Marble House today were there on August 19, 1892, when the Vanderbilts had a coming out party for their new "cottage."

The Gold Ballroom (facing page, above left, above right and overleaf) at Marble House (these pages and overleaf) is a masterpiece of decorative art. Its mantlepiece holds bronze figures of Youth and Old Age and a mask of Dionysus by J. Allard et Fils of Paris, who produced many other artifacts in the house, including chandeliers equipped for both electricity and gas, and the statuary in other parts of the ballroom. The carved wooden panels, depicting scenes from Greek and Roman mythology, are by sculptor Karl Bitter.

The dining room (above) at Marble House (these pages) is a copy of the Salon of Hercules at Versailles. Its pink Numidian marble walls support a portrait of Louis XIV. The Gothic Room (facing page bottom) and Mrs. Vanderbilt's sitting room (top) are less grand, but as exquisitely decorated, and the bedrooms are worthy of a palace.

The bookshelves, paneling and furniture in the library (facing page) of Marble House (these pages and overleaf) are of carved English walnut. The library panels represent the sciences and the frescoes are of Time and History. The dining room (above) is decorated with hunting and fishing scenes. After her divorce from Willie K. Vanderbilt in 1896, Alva married O.H.P. Belmont and went to work redesigning his Newport mansion, Belcourt. But perhaps her heart still lay in Marble House, where the music of times gone by lingers on in the Gold Ballroom (overleaf).

INDEX